How to Apply for Scholarships in

5

Easy Steps

Boss Edition

ALSO BY DR. LESLEY SCHARF

Contributing Essay Coach

How to Apply for Scholarships in

5

Easy Steps
Boss Edition

A Student's Guide to Applying for Scholarships

Shedly Casseus Parnther

Copyright © 2023, Shedly Casseus Parnther, M.B.A.

All rights reserved. No part of this publication may be reproduced, distributed, or transmitted in any form or by any means, including photocopying, recording, or other electronic or mechanical methods, without the prior written permission of the author. Unless otherwise expressed, all quotations and references must be permitted by Author.

For information regarding special discounts on bulk purchases of this book, charitable donations, or for speaking engagements, please visit my website thescholarshipplug.com, Facebook facebook.com/scholarshipmoneyforstudents, Instagram instagram.com/scholarshipmoneyforstudents/, YouTube youtube.com/c/TheScholarshipPlug, or Email via info@scholarshipplug.com

ISBN: 979-8-9866536-3-1

Designed & Published by JWG Publishing House. Printed in the United States of America.

What's Inside

Acknowledgment	1
My Why	6
This Book is for You	8
Where to Search for Scholarships	14
Affirmations	16
Introduction	17
Step 1 Make the Commitment and Get Organized Now	19
Step 2 Prepare	23
Sample Brag Sheet	30
Sample Resume'	32
Sample Tax Return	35
Steps to Writing Your Best Essay	42
Step 3 Set Targets, Schedule, and Track	48
Step 4 Find Your Plug	51
Step 5 Put Key People on Alert	55
The 100 Scholarship Challenge	59

What's Inside

Quick Tips	61
It's The Best time for a Side Hustle	63
Financial Freedom and Building Wealth as a Student	67
PRAISE Yourself	71
Tips not Myths	72
College Trackers	78
Scholarship Trackers	88
NOTES	98

Acknowledgment

This book would not have been possible without the support of several people, especially my family. Nobody has been more important to me in the pursuit of this project in its entirety than the members of my family. I would like to thank my awesome husband Brad, who has always believed in me and encouraged me to do what I'm passionate about. His love and guidance are with me in whatever I pursue.

Thank you to my children, Demitre, Myah, and Nathaniel who provide unending inspiration. Demitre, thanks for listening to me about securing scholarships early. As a result of following the proven steps in this guide, you were able to earn your first scholarship in the 7th grade. Now you are pursuing your college degree with scholarship money you received and more.

Myah, I'm grateful for your continuous belief in my vision. You are the sweetest daughter I can ever ask for; love you, beautiful. Thank you for assisting me with the inception of The Scholarship Plug Instagram page that is followed by students, educators, and parents around the world. You are bound for success in the health industry. Keep it up, Doc; you're almost there!

My youngest son, Nathaniel, who is always with me traveling from city to city as I conduct scholarship and college planning workshops, thank you. I know that from these workshops, you have garnered the experiential knowledge of the scholarship application process and the grit you will need to win in not only in pursuing what you want to do but in life. (If you need a new pair of Jordans, contact GLOBOKICKS.)

I'm especially grateful to my mother Genevieve, who instilled the value of education in my siblings and me. My late father, may you rest in heaven. I have become the businessperson you've always dreamt that I'd become! I miss and love you so much.

My sister Stichiz, my first official spokesperson who

always uses any and every opportunity to promote my vision, you are incredible at what you do, and your God-given talents will make a positive impact around the world forever! I wish our father were alive to witness all your accomplishments. My brother Edgar, you've always had my back even from a distance. Thank you for your infinite love. You love to support your family.

Shout out to True Tread Tires! (If you need tires be sure to call TRUE TREAD TIRES #954-479-8841 and tell them I sent you - a shameless plug) 😊

To my CC&C Consulting Group team. Ms. Yanique, Dr. Scharf, and Seya you already know, I couldn't do this without you. The firm literally runs because of you. Your expertise, skills, and energy go unmatched. Thank you for your heart, your time, and your dedication to the growth of the business. To the Scholarship Plug Board of Advisors, especially my friend Michelle Jones for the daily encouragement. Thank you all for believing in my vision without any doubt or hesitation and for offering your leadership to the success of the organization.

To my Casseus, Parnther & Fabien family, extended family, and to my friends whose love, care, and support means everything to me, you know who you are! Special thanks to my first book's editor, Ms. Suzanne Margolin; what a force of genius you are! I can never forget you. To the JWG publishing team at the JWG Publishing House, thank you for your expertise and for your team's patience in working with me on this project.

To my original Broward County Public School District family, Broward County BRACE Advisors, BRACE Cadets, Northeast High School family, School Counselors, FAU Upward Bound original staff, Broward College staff, Broward County Library staff and the Will Make It Family: There are no words to describe the sacrifice, effort, and time we all put into our students. Keep up the great work and keep pouring into the students the best way you can.

Special shout out to Uchicago and the Counselor Fly-In programs across the country. I wouldn't have had the chance to write book one if I were not presented with such a great opportunity to visit your institution. My passion to tour college campuses to share my experiences and knowledge with students has reached new heights. You've motivated me to continue and complete this scholarship guide for students and parents to use. I am proud to witness your success and progress as you continue the great work you do. I look forward to visiting several other college campuses and youth programs across the world to speak about scholarships.

Thank you!

My Why

In everything you do, it is important to have a clear understanding, or focus as to why you are doing what you are doing. The Florida Bright Futures Scholarship is a state scholarship program funded by The Florida Lottery for eligible graduating high school students. This scholarship program came out the year before I graduated high school, and I didn't complete the application. I honestly don't think I even considered taking advantage of it.

My "Why" originated from this: If I knew then what I know now, I would have dedicated more time applying for scholarships or retested over and over trying to earn the Florida Bright Futures Scholarship and I certainly never would have taken out as many student loans as I did. I know now that the extra guidance from a trusted educator could have made a massive difference in my financial life today. That is why my goal is to help you attend college with little to no financial obligation to you

- you could even be "paid" to go.

So great job taking the time to read **How to Apply for Scholarships in 5 Easy Steps**, a special guide & planner for students, created by me, your Scholarship Plug, Mrs. Shedly Casseus Parnther.

You are in the right place!

This Book is for You

If you are reading this, thank you. Here's why I want you – yes, YOU, to go to college and get paid for it.

If I came to you today and told you that I would pay for all your costs associated with you attending a college, I mean everything from paying your bills at home, your car, your books, your housing...everything! What college would you attend?

Write it down here: _____

Write today's date here: _____

Now we're on to something. I knew it.
Don't believe the hype.

Give yourself a chance to grow on another level and experience a new environment with new people that seek opportunity and self-awareness. You deserve it, and the effort you put in is a direct result of what you will receive. It's ok to not know what you want to major in right now but surrounding yourself with peers who aspire to be better people and advance their skills matters. Let's see if this book is intended just for you!

This Book Is for You

- ✓ You believe college is not possible because of your current financial position.
- ✓ The college you want to attend costs too much.
- ✓ You are a first-generation student, which means your parents did not earn a 4-year degree.
- ✓ You are a second-generation student, and your parents graduated a long time ago and don't understand the processes in place today.
- ✓ You are an international student.
- ✓ You identify as an undocumented student.
- ✓ You have doubts.
- ✓ You have low test scores.
- ✓ You have high test scores.
- ✓ You have a low grade-point average.
- ✓ You have a high grade-point average.
- ✓ You worked hard in high school.
- ✓ You wish you had worked harder in high school.

- ✓ You live in a single-parent household.
- ✓ You live with both parents.
- ✓ You've experienced trauma and are still working through it.
- ✓ You've witnessed someone you care about go through a traumatic experience.
- ✓ You have a disability.
- ✓ You have been told "no" before.
- ✓ You fear this entire college planning process.
- ✓ You feel alone.
- ✓ You wear glasses.
- ✓ You are different.
- ✓ You have earned at least one service hour.
- ✓ You've never met your birth parents.
- ✓ You've done something that you now regret.
- ✓ You have a parent who is a veteran.
- ✓ You have a grandparent who is a veteran.
- ✓ You want to go to college.
- ✓ You have been told that college is not for you.
- ✓ If you love God.

This book is for you! Keep reading.

I stress...

Does your doctor enter the patient's room without a stethoscope? Does a mechanic work on your car without their ratchet or wrench?

What about a teacher without a lesson plan? Or even social media influencers...can they share content without a social media platform?

Use the same theory for yourself.

Consider applying for scholarships like your own business.

You are the CEO and all the other key positions that a new business owner often takes on during the first phase of starting a business.

You are the CEO/founder in charge of prioritizing (this is your investment), the secretary who organizes, types, and follows up calls and emails, and the marketing manager, promoting your scholarship mission to everyone who can help you along the process. You are the product; you need to sell yourself.

Are you with me?

You are in the business of education, and it is your business to get your education paid for. Don't make this too personal. Keep it business!

Tools needed to maximize the opportunities to make getting paid to go to college possible includes:

- An unofficial and official transcript;
- Translated official transcript (if you are an international student);
- Student Aid Report;
- FAFSA;
- Acceptance letters or proof of enrollment (if applicable);
- Personal statement that includes why you deserve to be selected;
- Resumé
- Three letters of recommendations;
- Test scores: SAT, ACT, PSAT, etc.
- List of accomplishments;

- Five References (Full name, title, number, email, and the number of years known);

- College application trackers;

- Scholarship application trackers;

- Laptop or tablet;

- Gmail account;

- Google Docs;

- Copy of your student visa; and

*If you are an international student, be sure to have your documents officially translated by an approved translator in the language in which you plan on studying.

Where to Search for Scholarships

Brainstorm. There are scholarship opportunities for EVERYTHING. Start by making a list of all your strengths. Be mindful of the weaknesses that are your strengths in the world of scholarships. For example, you may think that having a low income is a weakness when it is a strength. Identifying as a low-income student can be an eligibility requirement for financial need-based scholarships.

Another example is if you have a disability. Many may mistake this as a weakness, when in fact it is a strength. There are specific scholarships that support students with disabilities; however, I am speaking about those that do not specifically require you to have a disability. That is your opportunity to include the fact that your disability is used to empower and conquer. Your disability is what sets you apart from other applicants applying for the same scholarship. Your disability is a strength!

Once you've created your list with all of your strengths, label it "My Strengths."

Now you can base your search on the categories based on your strengths. Do not limit yourself. Apply to as many scholarships as possible based on as many strengths... it's been done so many times that I know you can do it! You will thank yourself later.

I promise.

Affirmations

Repeat the following every day....

I am a successful college student.
My education will be paid for.
I can do this.
I will do this because I deserve it.
I am on the right track to a great life.
I am happy.
I am a person that helps make others happy.
I am loved.
I love myself.
I have the courage to take on anything that comes my way.
I create success.
My challenges will make me stronger as I overcome them.
Every day is an opportunity.

*Everything that manifests in the natural,
first starts in the mind............*

Introduction

I was standing in line at my favorite craft store when a young lady at the next register called out, "Excuse me!" I turned around, and she asked if I were the Scholarship Queen from Instagram. I couldn't help but smile as I replied, "Yes. Yes, I am actually. Thank you!" The young lady returned the grin and said, "I know you because I follow you!" I felt such excitement and thought about how incredible it was that people were actually paying attention to The Scholarship Plug on social media. (I can be a low-key dork sometimes.) I asked her which scholarship she was working on, and she answered, "I don't know how to apply."

My heart sank instantly. I made an expression, like, "What the heck was the point of following then?" before I told her to message me so that I could help get her on the right path. I needed to step up my game, before the next morning. The next morning on my fly-in trip to the University of Chicago, I resolved that I would create my first draft of an official scholarship guide, an easy read for all students and parents to follow each step. No more will I have a follower or a student within my reach that does not know how to apply for scholarships. I'm still waiting for that young lady's message.

This guide is dedicated to both the new and existing students, parents, family members, and community leaders that follow The Scholarship Plug pages on Instagram, Facebook, YouTube, Twitter, Snapchat, WhatsApp, Tik Tok, and LinkedIn, or keep up to date with www.TheScholarshipPlug.com. Thank you, again, for allowing me to guide you through this process. Commitment is one of the key ingredients needed to reach any goal. No matter how big or small in any aspect of your life, a commitment to yourself is a requirement! You are committing to supporting your education through scholarship money....

Make it happen!
We have no time to waste.
Let's get started!

STEP 1

Make the Commitment and Get Organized Now

Commit: You must genuinely commit to your quest for scholarship money. A fun way of achieving this is with my **100 Scholarship Challenge** - especially if you're competitive! I created the challenge to rouse students to take initiative and commit to applying to at least 100 scholarships before their graduation. In this way, you can keep yourself accountable. You can also commit by signing up on our website. There you will find sample documents and forms to help you with your scholarship process. It also has all the information posted on my social media pages specifically for those of you without social media.

Organize: Please designate a folder for scholarships only. Now designate a space where you will keep your folder and documents for scholarships.... Oh, I'm not joking. This is all part of the process; please do this now. Then, create two folders in your email. Label one 'Scholarship Docs' and the other, 'Scholarships to Do."

In the 'Scholarship Docs' folder, save all documents that will be used to complete your scholarships. In the "Scholarships to Do" folder, you'll save emails or packets that you receive related to any scholarship that you will be completing. Do this now. Then, get a USB flash drive. Create two folders on your drive and repeat the above process. As you get older you will realize that a strong, organized foundation means less time wasted, which will result in high-quality outcomes. **Keep in mind that a person can tell if your scholarship application was rushed vs if care was taken to deliver your best work.** There's a clear difference often identified immediately by a scholarship reviewer! "If you don't invest the time in creating the path for accomplishing your goals, you're pretty much laying out a goal that's not even worth investing your time into."

>
> ### Do this now. Please!
>
> Now, get a USB flash drive and create 2 folders on your drive.
>
> Again, label the first folder "Scholarship Docs" and the second "Scholarships To Do". Same deal, we are saving all the documents in the "Scholarship Docs" folder and any potential scholarship you are thinking of applying for in the "Scholarships To Do" folder.
>
> Do this now.
>
> "If you don't invest the time in creating the path for accomplishing your goals, you are pretty much laying out a goal that's not even worth investing your time into".
>
> As you get older you will realize that strong preparation means less time wasted which often results in quality product or work.
>
> **Keep in mind that a person can tell if your scholarship application was rushed vs if care was taken to deliver your best effort. There's a big difference!**

STEP 2

Prepare

The following items will make your goal much easier; I promise!

It is a fact that not all scholarships will require the same information. That being said, you may come across scholarships that only require you to answer their essay prompt. However, to make this scholarship system work, it is going to require you to be organized, focused, and equipped. Have you ever heard of an army attacking without their weapons? Do you go to class without a pen or pencil to take notes? Do you drive up to the drive-thru without your money to pay? Exactly! This is how you should prepare to apply for scholarships. Let's do this step by step.

You have seven days from today to obtain these documents. Ready?

Item #1- School Transcripts

Transcripts- This is a record of all your courses and received grades throughout your high school or college career (dual enrollment credits included). Request this today! If you are reading this on a weekend, put it in your calendar (with an alarm) to request a copy first thing Monday morning from your school's School Counseling Department. They will direct you. If they ask you why you need a transcript, tell them you are preparing to apply for scholarships! You need three copies of your official transcript. Your official transcript will be given to you in a sealed envelope. Ask the person who will be printing your transcript if they can also send you an electronic copy to you as a pdf file. If not, it's fine. Many schools do not offer this service.

Once you receive the transcripts, keep two of the three sealed copies in your scholarship document folder as we will need them later. Take one of the official transcripts, break the seal, open it and read it! You should see ALL the grades of your high school or college career. You want to make sure that all the information is correct (name, address, course grades, attendance, service hours, race, rank...) so check EVERYTHING.

This is officially your copy! If you were not able to receive an electronic copy from your School Counseling Department, then please scan all pages (front & back) of your transcripts.

Once you're done, go ahead and name it your first initial and last name dash transcript. [Example: S. Casseus-Transcript.] Send the scanned copy to yourself via email and move it to the "Scholarship Docs' folder. Now you can save the same transcript on your USB flash drive in your 'Scholarship Docs' folder. Are you still with me? Good. So now you have one saved document in both of your 'Scholarship Docs' folders.

Item #2 Letters of Recommendation

Letters of Recommendation. Letters of recommendation are letters that people familiar with your personal and academic accomplishments write on your behalf. They may also share experiences they've had with you. Letters of recommendation can come from different sources such as your teacher, coach, school counselor, college, and career advisor, manager, coworker, administrator, club advisor, local city, county, or state official, tutor, or non-profit organization representative.

Even the crossing guard of your school, who you have said "good morning" to for the past five years, is a good source for a letter of recommendation. Anyone who has had some type of experience or relationship with you and can attest to something you have done or overcome is a source for a letter of recommendation.

Allow at least two to three weeks for your recommenders to provide you with their letters. If you haven't heard from them after two weeks, send them a friendly email or phone reminder. Always say, "Please" and "Thank you"! Don't be afraid to follow up on your requests; it's not about bothering anyone; it's about getting what you need done as soon as possible. Don't make this personal. If they are not available to write one for you, move on to another recommender. Once you have your letters, scan your letters, save your letters and label them as your first initial last name, and Letter of Rec 1. [Ex: S. Casseus Letter of Rec 1]. Save them in your 'Scholarship Docs' folder in your email and save them to your drive.

Item #3- A List of Activities

A List of Activities. The following three items may seem repetitive but please trust me and follow my lead.

Student Activity Sheet

The purpose of the Student Activity Sheet is to provide detailed information to your teachers, administrator or counselor that he/she can utilize when writing your college recommendation. We encourage students to download this document from Danbury High School's Guidance Website (under "Forms") and type in your responses, then print, sign, and submit the Student Activity Sheet to either your teacher, administrator or counselor. This document is to be completed by the student. Please note that only your teacher, administrator or counselor will have access to this document.

Name of Student: _____

Cell Phone: _____ Email: _____

School Counselor: _____

My teacher, administrator or counselor, in his/her recommendation, may use any information I provide.

Student Signature: _____ Date: _____

Chronicling Your Involvements and Activities

Extracurricular: List any clubs or activities at Danbury High School or in the community in which you have been involved in order of importance to you. Please note any leadership roles and level of involvement.

Club Activity	Grade(s)	Position Held, Details and Accomplishments

Athletics: List each sport, level of participation (Freshman, Varsity, JV, or Club) and any special recognition you have received (Captain, All-Star, All-FCIAC, etc.).

Sport	Grade(s)	Position/Awards

First, take a few minutes to brainstorm on EVERYTHING you've accomplished, were involved in, worked for, and worked on. (Get your parents in on this if you need to, especially if you draw a blank.) Upload the list to a word doc that has the name of the activities, the time frame (months/years) during which you've participated, and a description of respon- sibilities. Be sure to include your leadership positions if you've held any. This is literally only a list; number it 1, 2, 3, 4, etc..

Here's an example:

1. "A" & "B" Honor Roll 9th-11th grade — "A" Honor roll recognized for academic excellence in the 1st and 2nd semester.
2. National Honor Society — Treasurer elected to manage monetary activities for the program and produce monthly reports to present to the board.
3. Fort Lauderdale Baptist Church — Youth Ministry Leader responsible for the curriculum during Bible study, establishing a welcoming environment for new and existing guests along with creating an effective membership follow-up system. Keep in

mind that you can always edit this list; just remember to always save it. You can refer to this when you are completing your college applications. If you don't have much to add, it's time to make some changes and get involved. Seriously and immediately! Print three copies. Save this list in your 'Scholarship Docs' folder in your email and on your drive as your Activities [S. Casseus Activities].

Item #4- A Brag Sheet

A brag sheet allows you to brag about yourself. You are giving as much information as possible to help your recommender write the best letter of recommendation possible. For a sample fill-in-the-blank.

My Brag Sheet

Hello,

Thank you for taking the time to write a letter of recommendation for me. As of today, I have committed to applying to 100 Scholarships. Below are a details about me that will help you put together the best possible letter of recommendation. I truly respect your time and appreciate your support.

My name is: _____
My email address is: _____
My phone number is: _____
I will graduate in (year): _____
I attend (school): _____
I plan on attending (college/university/tech school): _____
I plan on pursuing a career in: _____
My GPA is: _____
I have _____ hours of community service.
I spend most of my time: _____
My highest ACT score is: _____ My highest SAT score is: _____
My biggest goal in life is to: _____
_____
I enjoy: _____
_____
Words that describe me are: _____
I am a member of (clubs/programs/position): _____
_____
I've worked at: _____ for _____ hours per week.
Today's date is: _____ if you could please have your letter back to me by: _____ I would truly appreciate it. Thank you.

Need Scholarships?
#100ScholarshipChallenge

Item #5- A Scholarship Resumé

Now that you've completed items three and four, you are going to organize some of the information to create your scholarship resumé.

See sample resumé on the next page. You can also request a sample resumé by emailing us at info@scholarship.com. If your school uses Naviance, there is a resumé template feature that will allow you to enter your information and will generate your information in a complete resumé format for you. Done? Great. Save it, print five copies, and add it to your "Scholarship Docs" folder in your email and on your drive. Now we are ready for anything and everything upon demand. On to the next item.

Sample Resume

Mary Love

Scholarhill, FL 12345
954.456.7890
marylove123@gmail.com

Skills
- Effective Communication (writing and verbal)
- Strong Customer Service Skills
- Great Team Member
- Punctuality and Dependability
- Microsoft Office and Technology
- Fluent in Spanish and Chinese

Experience

Fish-fil-A / Team Member
June 2020 - Current   Fort Lauderdale, FL
Welcome & greet guests, take and prepare customer orders and maintained cleanliness in work and dining areas.

BMC Cinema / Guest Services Associate
January 2019 - June 2020   Davie, FL
Crossed trained in customer service ticket management and event planning. Responsible for answering guest questions, theatre movie locations and times. Coordinating and planning youth events and birthday parties to ensure a memorable experience.

Kids Club / Volunteer
January 2018 - Current   Lauderhill, FL
Assist Management with youth programs, answer parent questions, facilitate registration for holiday camps, promote volunteer programs to my peers for service hours opportunities, assist with scheduling.

Education & Involvement

Casseus High School / High School Diploma
Graduation : June 2023
Fort Lauderdale, FL 34015
GPA: 3.49
- **Advanced Placement Courses:** French, Biology and History
- **Clubs:** Debate Club, French Club, Dance Club
- **Church:** Active Youth Ministry Member
- **Enrichment:** Upward Bound College Prep Program
- **Sports:** Band, Tennis, Soccer & Basketball

Awards & Recognitions
- Nominated and Elected for Class Vice President
- Volunteer of the Year (for two consecutive years)
- Employee of the Month (October 2020, March 2021, July 2022)
- Top 15% of the Class

References are available upon request

Item #6- Your Personal Statement

No two scholarship programs are created equal; therefore, you can expect the requirements to be different. However, most of the scholarship programs are going to require similar documents to determine if you are a good fit for their scholarship program by asking you to tell them a little more about who you are. Tell ALL!

What should they know about you besides your grades and involvement? Who are you? Discuss your obstacles, what makes you different, and what attributes you bring to the table. Keep it under 750 words and above 250 words. This may not come naturally so give yourself some time to brainstorm on why you should be selected to receive a scholarship! Seek help for this one. See page 25 for a guide on how to draft a winning scholarship essay.

This document will take more time than some others, but the good news is once you have a winning personal statement you may be able to reuse, edit, cut, paste and use it again. When you have completed your first draft, read it out loud to yourself, make the necessary edits, save it and print three copies.

Now give a copy to your teacher or club sponsor, someone you trust that may have sound editing skills, and a friend. When you get your edited draft, make the corrections, save them, label it "Personal Statement" (i.e.: S. Casseus Personal Statement), and add it to your 'Scholarship Docs' folder, both in your email and on your drive. Remember each scholarship has a different essay prompt for you to write about. If the essay prompt asks you to answer a specific topic unrelated to your personal statement, then send it.

Item #7- A Student Aid Report from FAFSA

This task is for 11th graders and up! This item is important because it will immediately let you know how much Federal Aid money you may be eligible to receive. To get this information, you are going to have to complete your FAFSA, the Free Application for Student Aid. If you haven't completed your FAFSA, if you do not have a social security number, or if you are not an eligible noncitizen - STOP- and seek help from your college advisor or counseling department to complete the application now.

If you do not qualify or are not sure if you qualify for Federal Aid, please consult with your college advisor or counseling department or message us on The Scholarship Plug about your situation. Whether you believe you qualify for need- based aid or not, complete the application. Many scholarships from your college depend on this application. There are even scholarships for those who don't qualify for FAFSA dollars because of family income, but universities and colleges must have that application for you to be considered.

After you have completed the FAFSA in three to five business days you will have access to your Student Aid Report (SAR). We need this. Save it and label it with your first initial and last name dash SAR. Save it to your 'Scholarship Docs' folder in your email and your drive.

The College Board's CSS Profile (College Scholarship Service Profile), is another financial aid application your college or university may ask you to complete. You may find the application tedious, but it is worth it in the end. This application allows institutions to determine how much "more" in grants and scholarships you may be eligible for.

Item #8- A Tax Return and W2's - optional

A tax return is a federal report filed by income earners that documents your parent's annual income. This report is used to file annual income taxes. Why do you need this? Many scholarship programs will use the information on the tax return to determine if you qualify for the financial need requirement.

How To Apply For Scholarships In 5 Easy Steps

A W2 is a document given to an employee at the beginning of each year. It displays how much income a person earned in the previous calendar year and is issued by an employer(s). There will be multiple W2's if you or your parents work more than one job. Tip: I can say this 100 times. Whether you believe you qualify or not, use whatever income information you have; you must complete the application. These are all important and sensitive documents. Your family may or may not allow you to have a copy or the original for that matter. If you are trusted with these documents then make a copy of your parent's taxes, black out the social security #'s on the copy, scan it and save it as "Parent Taxes." File it away in your 'Scholarship Docs' folder. Don't forget to do the same for yourself if you filed taxes.

Item #9- A Professional Headshot

More and more scholarship programs are requesting a wallet-size headshot of you. Headshots may be taken at your local convenience store or photography company; you can use your yearbook picture from your school (ask your administrator how to obtain it,) or maybe you know someone with a nice camera. Even the latest smartphone cameras aren't too bad, but you want to ensure that it is a headshot, from your chest up, with professional attire. Be well groomed and use a standard solid background.

Always ask for an electronic jpeg. or png. copy so that you can save it in your 'Scholarship Docs' folder. Also, have up to five photocopies available to send off.

> **Tip 1:** When calling a photography company, say something like this: "I'm preparing to apply for scholarships to go to college and several scholarship programs will ask me for a wallet sized headshot. Are you able to please help me with that?"

> **Tip 2:** Schools usually have picture day every year to update IDs and for use in the upcoming yearbook. Make this year's picture day a professional picture and dress accordingly. You can use this picture for scholarships.

Item #10- A Book of Stamps

A book of stamps is a small booklet with twenty stamps and will run you about $12+. This is for old-fashioned scholarship programs. You are going to need stamps to put on your envelopes when mailing out scholarship documents. Be sure to check how many stamps are needed for your package. A good idea is to take it to the post office for an accurate weight and they will tell you the right number of stamps to put on your package. The worst is when you have completed a scholarship application, have gathered all the documents, and mailed it, only to find out later that it has been returned because you didn't use enough stamps. Trust me; I've had students that learned the hard way.

> **Tip**: If you can't get to the post office, ask an adult to "over guesstimate" if you have the right number of stamps on the envelope based on the weight of the package.

Item #11- Manila Envelopes

A manila envelope is a mustard- colored envelope that usually seals with a clasp and has a sticky film on the flap. A good size to purchase is a ten by thirteen [10x13]. You will use these envelopes for those scholarships that require you to mail in your documents.

Purchase at least fifteen to twenty envelopes to be sure you have plenty on hand for now. Your envelope should have Stamps (around three to five), the address where it's going, and your address.

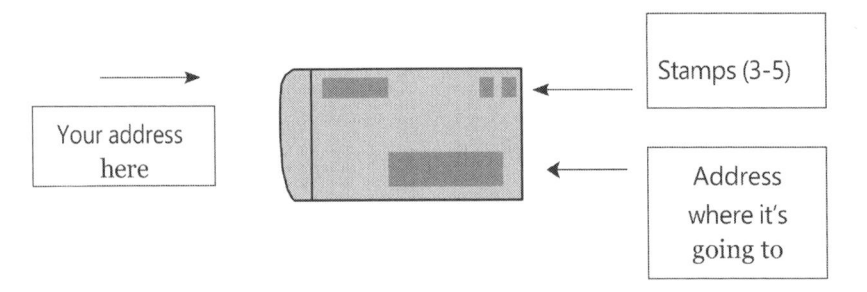

```
                            ┌──────────────┐
      ──────▶  ┌────────┐   │ Stamps (3-5) │
 ┌──────────┐  │        │◀──└──────────────┘
 │Your address│ │        │
 │   here    │  │        │   ┌──────────────┐
 └──────────┘  │        │◀──│  Address      │
               └────────┘   │  where it's   │
                            │  going to     │
                            └──────────────┘
```

Item #12- A Student Contact Card

Oh yes! By the time we are done, you are going to be a "Professional Scholarship Applier." I am not joking!

Businesspeople or professionals call this item a business card. If you thought, you were too young to make yourself a business card you are wrong. You are going to create a business card to show people that you are not playing games about your education right now. You can use any template to create a business card. I have provided a student card template on my website.

It can be as fancy or as plain as you'd like. Make it represent you! Save it in your 'Scholarship Docs' folder. Then, print and cut out fifty cards and keep them in an envelope so that they stay fresh, clean, and neat. You can use plain paper or card stock. A standard student card will include your first and last name, phone number, and email address. You may also include your graduation year if you'd like.

Below is a sample:

> ## Shedly Casseus Parnther
> Class of 20??
>
> Email: info@scholarshipplug.com
> Phone: 954-951-2175
>
> 100 Scholarship Challenge participant

Now that you are done you should have a "Scholarship Docs" file on your drive and in your email account. You also have all your hard-copy documents in a folder in that safe place in your home. You are now ready for any and everything! If there is an on-the-spot scholarship opportunity you are beyond ready!

Steps to Writing Your Best Essay
By Contributing Author
Dr. Lesley Scharf

Writing the best essay can open the door to success!

Writers love to write about writing. But the truth is, producing a masterpiece or even a paragraph that effectively says what you want it to say is not always easy. Whether you are a good writer or one who says, "I'm just not good at writing," you can always improve. Steps can be taken towards being the best writer you can be.
Set a goal. Include a due date and reason for setting that goal.

Make a commitment. Promise yourself you can and will complete the task, whether it involves writing a letter, completing an application, or drafting an essay. Make up a mantra, a statement such as, "I will finish my essay by Friday," and post it where you will see it. Repeat it often. Saying it can increase the probability of it happening.

Remember writing is a process. Oh, I know some of you will say. "I just write, and my essay comes out fine." You may be a talented writer, but you may do even better proofreading and editing, so give yourself time.

Time? Yes, free from distractions as much as possible. Turn off the tv even if it is a reality show providing "background noise." Consider soothing music instead if quiet doesn't work for you. You need time for each part of the writing process.

- Thinking/planning
- Writing the rough draft
- Reviewing, editing, and revising the draft
- Writing and rewriting
- Final editing and revising
- Stepping aside to revisit it before that ultimate goal
- Publication: The ultimate goal (which may include submitting, sending, printing, and sharing it).

So that's the process. Now, PLAN.

Be aware of who is evaluating the work, reading your application, and/or sponsoring the scholarship. That can give you an idea of what direction to take with the writing.

Read and identify keywords in the prompt, in the question, or the assignment. Watch out for questions that give you a choice. If you are asked to write about dogs, cats, or birds, "or" means choose just one animal!

Think about what you know and what you might need to research and consider further. You must be the authority, and if you are writing a personal essay or a narrative about yourself, YOU ARE the expert. Decide what you want to include in your writing. Make an idea list or an outline for yourself. Then see what you will write about first, second, third....

Note any special rules, such as word limit (and watch expressions like ". in an essay of at least 500 words," "in an essay no more than 500 words," or in "250-500 words").

Yes, readers do look at writers' ability to follow rules. It's easy to get a word count and easy to be disqualified for not following rules.

SPECIAL NOTE: Remember the word limit but don't worry if your first draft is too long. Like the suit jacket that can't always be let out or expanded but is always able to be altered by being "taken in," it is easier to condense and shorten what you've written than it is to lengthen an essay.

Go for it! Write your first draft. Get started ASAP! But wait; do you remember the structure of an essay?

Like everything in life, writing requires a beginning, a middle, and an end. The beginning, like the first quarter of a game, like the beginning of a date, like the grand opening of a restaurant, must make a good impression. If the spectator or participant, diner or audience (reader) does not have their attention "grabbed," or sees or tastes or reads something that is not up to their expectations, you have lost already. Avoid beginning with, "Hello, my name is Dr. Scharf and I have a story to tell." "I have a story," gets to the point faster. Is it interesting? Some essays begin with a quotation, a question posed, an observation or lesson learned, or an "in the past, now, and in the future approach," for example.

After you've grabbed the readers' attention and made them want to read further, be sure to mention at least key words in the prompt and try to end the first part of your essay with at least three points to be covered in the middle of your essay, the "body." Show you are on topic and give a preview of what points will be covered in the rest of your essay.

The middle, or the body of your essay is where you explain, describe, support, and elaborate on those points. If you get to the body and have run out of ideas, go back and make sure your introduction has points enough to expand in the body. Still stuck? Discuss your ideas with a friend or family member or someone who shares your interests, someone who knows you. Ask what they think. Share your thoughts and maybe a talk might get you thinking further. It's also sometimes helpful to ask yourself questions – "Why do I feel that way?" "What have I heard or experienced that makes me believe that?" "What could happen if, or what should be considered next?"

Back to the body, think of elaborating or explaining or building your essay as a way to build your case, to draw in the readers so they are following your thoughts. Show you have something to say! The reader should clearly see your ideas and be able to bullet them, listing them without struggling to sift through fluff (wordiness and needless repetition, aka "redundancy").

You've held the reader's attention, and you've elaborated and given support for your ideas, so now don't drop the ball just before crossing the goal line. Don't run off the stage before the curtain closes. Your conclusion should not seem rushed or not quite finished, as if you ran out of gas a few blocks from home. You spent time on the introduction and the body, and you should give the conclusion a power punch.

You could use strategies such as summarizing and restating the final, most important thought, tying ideas together with a relevant quote, posing a question, or challenging the reader to connect personally to what has been said within the essay. Above all, as your final statement, your closing argument, it should make a memorable impression, rousing the reader to shout out and cheer, fist bump, erupt in thunderous applause, and ultimately an "Amen!"

Now use the steps discussed and write about why you deserve a scholarship.

On to Step 3.

SHEDLY CASSEUS PARNTHER

STEP 3

Set Targets, Schedule and Track

Step 3- Set Targets, Schedule, and Track

I call this step the **TST** system. In this step, you are going to use the scholarship tracker provided at the end of this pamphlet or you can download a scholarship tracker on www.TheScholarshipPlug.com.

Just as in Step 2 where you had to prepare your items, here you are going to prepare your tasks and actions.

> *"There's a direct correlation between production and results. Do nothing, get nothing! Do more, get more!"*

Start with **T**, setting your **TARGETS**. Say your college is $34,000 per year and you have zero money, but they are offering you an extra $5,000 per year in institutional aid, plus FAFSA is awarding yours x $4,000 in Pell grant. This means you now need $25,000 in scholarship money. **THAT IS YOUR TARGET x4**. Write this amount at the top of each tracker so that you are reminded every time that this is what you must earn, and you are going to do whatever it takes to apply to as many scholarships until you reach this amount!

Then, **S, SCHEDULE** specific directions or tasks that you

must do at that particular date and time. Here's an example: In November I will complete four scholarships, one every Saturday. In December, I'll complete three scholarships every other Monday.

What is your scholarship schedule? Put it on the calendar on your cell phone and set a reminder alarm for yourself. Note: If you do not follow these instructions, this system will not work. Keeping a record or **T, Tracking** is a record of a specific task, action, or result. At the end of this guide you have scholarship application trackers, (front and back) to track eight different scholarships per page. Turn to the Tracker section to view your scholarship tracker. From now on, you will write down every scholarship you are working on or plan to complete.

For example, you would first write down your target scholarship amount that you'd need to have all costs to attend your college next to My Scholarship Goal $ box. Then enter the name of the scholarship, the value, when you are starting, the due date and then later on you will return to your tracker to update the status. Please use a pencil.

On to Step 4!

STEP 4

Find Your Plug

I'm going to be honest with you. I try to post on Instagram, Facebook, Twitter, WhatsApp, Snap Chat, Tik Tok and LinkedIn almost every day, if not every other day, and I am overwhelmed by all the information and scholarships that are available. I sometimes say to myself, I don't even know which one to post today because it's so much! So, I can imagine how you feel when you are looking at hundreds of scholarships to choose from.

> "You must control what you're taking in; that is why you are going to be selective as to which sources you are going to use as your primary scholarship sources."

Take one hour to research different scholarship sources and find out about scholarships or grants for which you may already qualify. Many programs guarantee scholarship money based on your grades, test scores, community service hours, and specific advanced placement courses. Find the money that is already yours!

Now it's your job to submit the requirements by the deadline. Do this: Call your state Department of Financial Aid to confirm if a scholarship program exists for students like yourself. Now call your county's community outreach office, your school district counseling office, and then your city office. These are usually funded by tax dollars or raised by local taxpayers anyway! Claim what is yours. Now, there are hundreds of scholarship sources but your goal here is to find a source that best fits you. If your school offers Naviance, there is a scholarship list that you may access. If your school offers a scholarship bulletin, then that may be a good source for you. Your counseling office, district website, and state financial aid site have lists and, of course, you can always follow my pages.

As you come across scholarships to which you want to apply, be sure to save them in your "Scholarships to Do" folder in your email and on your USB drive. Check this folder every day. Make it a habit! Decide on which three scholarship sources you are going to use, then apply the TST system. You can switch out scholarship sources if you feel that one of the sources is not what you expected! Remember, you are in control. Select the best fit for you! Here's another "plug" that a friend of mine does with his students.

Many high schools across the country host a Senior Awards Night to recognize those students who've earned scholarships. Awards may range from monetary scholarships to continuing their education or a trophy/certificate of recognition for their hard work and commitment through out their high school career.
Get your hands on the most recent year's program, read over ALL the awards and find out if any of those scholarships are or will be available for you to apply to. Easy!
Don't make this complicated.

Let's go, Step 5...

STEP 5

Put Key People on Alert!

In addition to committing to applying for scholarships as you did in Step 1, you are now adding people to your accountability circle and putting them on alert. Put at least two people on alert and let them know you are applying for scholarships. Examples of great people to put on your scholarship team are your teacher(s), school counselor, college advisor, employer, and your parent(s) or guardian(s). Ask them to let you know when they happen to come across a scholarship that might be a good fit for you. Explain that they can email, text, or share a picture of it with you on social media. This means that you are checking your emails religiously.

Remember that as you receive potential scholarships, save them in your "Scholarships to Do" folder in your email. Your statement can be something like this: "Hi, I want to let you know that I am on the hunt for scholarship money, (with a smile), so if you know of any scholarships or come across any scholarships that you think I may qualify for, please let me know! You can contact me via text or email. Here is my information!" Give them your student contact card and email them a copy of your resumé and brag sheet. **BAM!** You've already left an incredible impression!

Now you are ready to apply for scholarships!
1. Go to your <u>plug</u>.
2. <u>Identify</u> a scholarship.
3. <u>Read</u> the eligibility requirements.
4. Find the link or download and print the application on the site to apply.

If you meet the requirements - great! If not, move on to the next scholarship until you find one to do. Remember to write it down on your scholarship tracker. Some scholarships may be a good fit, while others may not be; if not, move on and keep applying. Don't wait for a response.

Keep it moving! There are too many scholarships for which to apply, for you to look back and wait for a response! You have this under control!

Feel free to contact me if you have any questions or

concerns. I pray that God continues to bless you and encourage you to pursue as much money as possible to pay for your entire education. Be sure to leave a comment or a review on the website or any of my social media pages. Especially if you've won a scholarship- message me. I would love to hear your thoughts about the information I've just provided to you and how it worked for you. I will be sure to personally respond.

Thank you for reading and/or listening to my step-by-step guide to applying for scholarships. I'm very excited for you. Now, go get that money!

The 100 Scholarship Challenge

The 70 Scholarship Challenge now called the 100 Scholarship Challenge was inspired by one of my first-generation high school juniors, Sabrina, who was determined to earn scholarships to pay for her college.

This student knew there was no other way for her to attend her dream college. To make a long story short, the student ended up having three times more than what she needed to attend the college of her dreams. Sabrina successfully completed and submitted 70+ scholarship applications between her junior and senior year in high school. It's almost like she made a career out of applying for scholarships. Sabrina graduated high school with not only enough scholarship money to pay her tuition and fees, but also enough to cover housing and books. Yet, she still had thousands of dollars left over to cover the rest of her undergraduate career! After I witnessed this journey, it set a new bar and new expectations, and it motivated me to keep pushing my students towards applying for as many scholarships as they could.

Sabrina was one of many that year to complete multiple scholarship applications. If Sabrina can make it happen, other students can do it! Guess what? She did NOT earn the Bright Futures Scholarship. So, there's no reason you cannot accomplish the same success. Not one reason! You deserve the same opportunity. Fast forward to today, and we have the 100 Scholarship Challenge! I rounded the number up to 100 because, well, why not? Everything is better at 100% (my cousin, Jaime of ATG Print House, pointed that out to me). My challenge to you is to commit to applying to 100 scholarships starting now until you reach the goal.

You are committing to do your absolute best to earn as much scholarship money as you possibly can. Psych yourself up and commit to applying to 100 Scholarships by going on the website and taking the challenge. Click on the "Take the Challenge" button and complete the form so that we have your information to keep you motivated via email or text. You can never be too young or too old to apply for scholarships. For those of you who are younger than eighteen years old, be sure to include your parent's information. Are you currently in college? Take the challenge and get those scholarship dollars while you can. Identify your first scholarship and write it down on your official scholarship tracker.

Once you have completed your 100th scholarship application, submit your tracking sheets to us for your 100 Scholarship Challenge gift package which includes an official Scholarship Plug certificate. Are you up for the challenge? Go for it! I believe in YOU!

Quick Tips

- Make copies if you can of each scholarship application that you complete.

- Watch for deadlines and set reminders in your phone calendar.

- Memorize your TST system (Targets/Schedule/Track).

- Attend Scholarship, FAFSA, and College Planning workshops. There's always something new to learn. You can never attend too many.

- Engage your parents or a guardian that you trust. (You are going to need a team).

- Don't be afraid to ask someone for help. If you get rejected, "No" is a full sentence. Move on to the next person.

- Stay in touch with your college's financial aid and

admissions office. They will have scholarship opportunities for you when you are admitted!

- Stay organized by keeping your documents and scholarships in your scholarship folders.

- Stay organized by setting a time and place to do your scholarship applications.

- Keep track of who you need documents from (Recommenders) and set reminders as to when to follow up with them.

- Find out about your state, county, or city scholarship programs and what is needed to meet the requirements.

- Remember that there are scholarships for tuition, housing, books, transportation, food, fees, study abroad programs, internships, school supplies, dorm supplies, prom dresses, and more. Don't just focus on one type of scholarship.

- You are one person with many attributes.

- Know your costs to fully attend your college. Plan for the worst-case scenario x 4.

It's The Best time for a Side Hustle

I started my first business at the age of thirteen. Ms. Carol mentored me from her home as she ran her private boutique. Ms. Carol always told me that I had an advantage by being so young because people would be more encouraged to support a young person with ambition, a plan, and the guts to ask for a sale.

Fast forward to today, and the same holds for you. Go for the sale! If one person (outside of your family) will pay for it, then there's a strong possibility that others will do the same. Here are a few ideas that you may want to consider earning extra income while in school.

The following suggestions may have age restrictions. Supervision may be required. Be sure to consult or get approval from your parent or guardian if you are under age.

1. Obtain a work-study job if you are in college.
2. Apply to be a summer intern or after-school mentor if you are in high school.
3. Walk dogs.
4. Be a social media manager.

5. Design flyers.
6. Tutor online.
7. Consider having a driver service.
8. Be a grocery shopper.
9. Organize homes.
10. Organize offices.
11. Write blogs and sell ad spaces to local businesses.
12. Serve as a tour guide.
13. Complete online surveys.
14. Be a hairdresser's assistant.
15. Be a barber's assistant
16. Obtain a certification while in high school for a trade.
17. Rent out your car.
18. Offer advertising space on your car (if you are always driving).
19. Rent out space in your apartment or home.
20. See products on shopping apps.
21. Sell t-shirts.
22. Edit photos.
23. Sell handmade crafts.

24. Cook for busy families.
25. Offer music lessons.
26. Detail cars.
27. Create a course and sell it.
28. Design websites.
29. Referee youth sports teams.
30. Coach for youth sports teams.
31. Become a lifeguard.
32. Offer swim lessons.
33. Become a Notary and offer your services (18+).
34. Create logos for new companies.
35. Review essays for students.
36. Become an influencer on social media and offer ad space to businesses.
37. Create an Amazon store.
38. Learn, gather, and sell BLAK (Business Leaders Answer Kits).

Contact us about how you can earn by selling BLAK!

Go to www.thescholarshipplug.com/shop

Financial Freedom and Building Wealth as a Student

What does that even look like? I'll give you an example: One of my students started her application process with zero money and graduated with over $30,000 in her savings and zero debt. She is now preparing to purchase her first property. How did she do it? Hmmm... keep reading.

Applying early is key! To make a long story short, that student had zero money and her parents had no money to even pay for her applications. "No problem" is what I love to say when I know that funds are the least of our concerns at this point. I educated her on the waiver process and how her application fees can be waived. She took this information and ran with it as she was determined to go to college by any means possible. This student applied I think, two months before the priority deadline, submitted her supporting documents, and was accepted (keyword) EARLY. She was later offered an institutional scholarship from the university to attend.

Valerie (name has been changed for privacy purposes) worked hard for her grades and although her test scores did not quite meet the minimum requirements to attend various state schools at the time, she didn't let her shortcomings bring her down or keep her from moving forward. Valerie was persistent in learning more about the financial aid process as she needed more funds to cover all of her expenses because she was NOT staying home, and she WAS going to college.

Fast forward, Valerie dedicated her senior year in high school and continued during her transition to college to apply for as many scholarships as she could get her hands on despite her busy schedule. Her busy schedule consisted of a part- time job, accumulating profits which she consistently contributed to her savings in addition to creating a side hustle to earn more income as she was talented with braiding hair.

Valerie did not only make use of her time by braiding hair for her college peers, but she also continued to work her part-time job, managed her courses, and applied for more scholarships. Twenty-four hours a day! Where there is a will, there is always a way (Einstein). I dedicate an entire chapter to ideas on how you can generate multiple streams of income while being a student. The key is time management and prioritizing what is important to stay focused on your end goals.

By graduation, Valerie had saved over $30,000, was debt free, and is now working for a reputable Fortune 500 company, preparing to purchase her very first property with a plan to purchase a second property in three years. I chose to share her success story out of many because that was not an easy journey. Valerie fought for where she is now, and you can do it, too.

Although I encourage you to start ways of earning multiple streams of income, wealth is not all about earning money. It's also healthy! Without your health, you technically cannot accomplish everything you dream of accomplishing. Wealth includes self-care such as taking mental breaks, eating properly (staying away from junk food!), keeping yourself groomed, exercising regularly, spending time with family, taking trips, and exploring different places around the world.

Should getting enough sleep be included?

"There is no better time to get this experience than as a student, so take advantage of this time to make it happen."

PRAISE Yourself:

P - Be around good positive people that can uplift you and you do the same for others.

R - Raise your credit. Make it a goal to be in the upper 700's-800's.

A- Health is Wealth. Promote good health for yourself.

I - Stay faithful and pray. God is so good guys! You were not made to be unsuccessful or unhappy. Stay faithful and focused and he will deliver on his promise.

S - Self-care. It's ok to treat yourself from time to time.

E - Earn money! There's no better time to start earning, saving, and investing.

Tips Not Myths:

1. Complete the FAFSA. This is the Free Application for Federal Student Aid, regardless of if you think you qualify or not.

2. Create your personal support team.

3. Craft an unsigned letter of recommendation for yourself. Use this to share with potential recommenders so that they have a guide.

4. Draft a personal statement. Include why you deserve to be selected for a scholarship.

5. Follow four to five active social media platforms that share scholarship information. Social media can be consuming. Consume for a purpose and make scholarship and college information a priority while scrolling.

6. Avoid including your social security number on public forms. If it is required, to contact the scholarship program, ask if you can provide your

social security number only if selected.

7. Keep copies of all scholarship documents and applications. You may be able to recycle the information for a future scholarship throughout your college career.

8. Add every scholarship to your scholarship tracker in this book.

9. Add every college to your college tracker in this book.

10. Keep a record of all the sponsoring scholarship organizations that relate to your industry. Keep in contact with them and offer to be a volunteer. This may lead to a potential internship.

11. Read your essay aloud to a family or friend for feedback.

12. Sensitive information in your essay doesn't have to be specific. Keep it general enough to convey your message and support your point with a strong conclusion.

13. Try your best not to submit your application minutes before the deadline. It has happened many times that the application site crashes right before the deadline.

14. Apply for 100 scholarships. I challenge you to 100 scholarships.

15. Do not spend your time filling out scholarships that do not require an essay. I'd rather you spend time focusing on a strong essay first.

16. Write the total amount you need to go to college for the number of years you plan on attending.

17. Don't be afraid to brag about yourself. This is the time to tastefully brag about yourself!

18. Do not avoid the scholarships that offer $100, $200, and $500! Do you know how much one book costs??? Everything counts.

19. Educate yourself by attending scholarship training and workshops.

20. Stick to your scholarship schedule.

21. Do not leave anything blank. Complete or add any supporting documents if asked.

22. If it's an option, do it!

23. Yes, you can use a previous essay for another essay but be mindful of the prompt. It has to make sense. Remember to remove the name of the college, scholarship program, etc., before submitting a recycled essay.

24. Speak it into existence. You will win scholarships to pay for college! Better yet, get paid to go to college.

25. You got this! This has been done millions of times - why can't you do it, too?

Let's goooooo!

Are you up for the challenge? Go for it, I believe in YOU!

In pencil

- College Name: Write the college you plan or have applied for here.
- Total Cost: Write the TOTAL cost to attended each college.
- Status: Write your progress (not started, in progress or submitted).
- Decision: Pending, Accepted, Denied.

My College Tracker

University/College Name	Full Cost to Attend the College per Year	Date Submitted	Application Status	Descision
Sample College	$38,886.00	12/20/20XX	Completed	Awaiting

THE SCHOLARSHIP PLUG

www.thescholarshipplug.com/join-now

My College Tracker

University/College Name	Full Cost to Attend the College per Year	Date Submitted	Application Status	Descision
Sample College	$38,886.00	12/20/20XX	Completed	Awaiting

THE SCHOLARSHIP PLUG

www.thescholarshipplug.com/join-now

My College Tracker

University/College Name	Full Cost to Attend the College per Year	Date Submitted	Application Status	Decision
Sample College	$38,886.00	12/20/20XX	Completed	Awaiting

www.thescholarshipplug.com/join-now

My College Tracker

THE SCHOLARSHIP PLUG

University/College Name	Full Cost to Attend the College per Year	Date Submitted	Application Status	Decision
Sample College	$38,886.00	12/20/20XX	Completed	Awaiting

www.thescholarshipplug.com/join-now

My College Tracker

University/College Name	Full Cost to Attend the College per Year	Date Submitted	Application Status	Descision
Sample College	$38,886.00	12/20/20XX	Completed	Awaiting

www.thescholarshipplug.com/join-now

My College Tracker

University/College Name	Full Cost to Attend the College per Year	Date Submitted	Application Status	Decision
Sample College	$38,886.00	12/20/20XX	Completed	Awaiting

THE SCHOLARSHIP PLUG

www.thescholarshipplug.com/join-now

My College Tracker

University/College Name	Full Cost to Attend the College per Year	Date Submitted	Application Status	Descision
Sample College	$38,886.00	12/20/20XX	Completed	Awaiting

www.thescholarshipplug.com/join-now

My College Tracker

University/College Name	Full Cost to Attend the College per Year	Date Submitted	Application Status	Decision
Sample College	$38,886.00	12/20/20XX	Completed	Awaiting

www.thescholarshipplug.com/join-now

My College Tracker

University/College Name	Full Cost to Attend the College per Year	Date Submitted	Application Status	Descision
Sample College	$38,886.00	12/20/20XX	Completed	Awaiting

www.thescholarshipplug.com/join-now

My College Tracker

University/College Name	Full Cost to Attend the College per Year	Date Submitted	Application Status	Descision
Sample College	$38,886.00	12/20/20XX	Completed	Awaiting

www.thescholarshipplug.com/join-now

To-Do List

My Scholarship Tracker

My Scholarship $ Goal $

Scholarship Name	Amount of Scholarship	Start Date	Due Date	Awarded (Yes, No, TBA)
Tu Es Belle Scholarship	$ 1,000.00	2/16/20xx	5/1/20xx	TBA

www.thescholarshipplug.com/join-now

To-Do List

My Scholarship Tracker

My Scholarship $ Goal: $

Scholarship Name	Amount of Scholarship	Start Date	Due Date	Awarded (Yes, No, TBA)
Tu Es Belle Scholarship	$ 1,000.00	2/16/20xx	5/1/20xx	TBA

www.thescholarshipplug.com/join-now

My Scholarship Tracker

My Scholarship $ Goal: $

Scholarship Name	Amount of Scholarship	Start Date	Due Date	Awarded (Yes, No, TBA)
Tu Es Belle Scholarship	$ 1,000.00	2/16/20xx	5/1/20xx	TBA

To-Do List

www.thescholarshipplug.com/join-now

My Scholarship Tracker

My Scholarship $ Goal: $

Scholarship Name	Amount of Scholarship	Start Date	Due Date	Awarded (Yes, No, TBA)
Tu Es Belle Scholarship	$ 1,000.00	2/16/20xx	5/1/20xx	TBA

To-Do List

www.thescholarshipplug.com/join-now

How To Apply For Scholarships In 5 Easy Steps

My Scholarship Tracker

My Scholarship $ Goal: $

Scholarship Name	Amount of Scholarship	Start Date	Due Date	Awarded (Yes, No, TBA)
Tu Es Belle Scholarship	$ 1,000.00	2/16/20xx	5/1/20xx	TBA

To-Do List

www.thescholarshipplug.com/join-now

My Scholarship Tracker

My Scholarship $ Goal: $

Scholarship Name	Amount of Scholarship	Start Date	Due Date	Awarded (Yes, No, TBA)
Tu Es Belle Scholarship	$ 1,000.00	2/16/20xx	5/1/20xx	TBA

To-Do List

www.thescholarshipplug.com/join-now

How To Apply For Scholarships In 5 Easy Steps

My Scholarship Tracker

My Scholarship $ Goal: $

Scholarship Name	Amount of Scholarship	Start Date	Due Date	Awarded (Yes, No, TBA)
Tu Es Belle Scholarship	$ 1,000.00	2/16/20xx	5/1/20xx	TBA

THE SCHOLARSHIP PLUG

www.thescholarshipplug.com/join-now

To-Do List

My Scholarship Tracker

My Scholarship $ Goal: $

Scholarship Name	Amount of Scholarship	Start Date	Due Date	Awarded (Yes, No, TBA)
Tu Es Belle Scholarship	$ 1,000.00	2/16/20xx	5/1/20xx	TBA

www.thescholarshipplug.com/join-now

To-Do List

My Scholarship Tracker

My Scholarship $ Goal: $

Scholarship Name	Amount of Scholarship	Start Date	Due Date	Awarded (Yes, No, TBA)
Tu Es Belle Scholarship	$ 1,000.00	2/16/20xx	5/1/20xx	TBA

To-Do List

www.thescholarshipplug.com/join-now

To-Do List

My Scholarship Tracker

My Scholarship $ Goal: $

Scholarship Name	Amount of Scholarship	Start Date	Due Date	Awarded (Yes, No, TBA)
Tu Es Belle Scholarship	$ 1,000.00	2/16/20xx	5/1/20xx	TBA

www.thescholarshipplug.com/join-now

NOTES

How To Apply For Scholarships In 5 Easy Steps

Shedly Casseus Parnther

How To Apply For Scholarships In 5 Easy Steps

Shedly Casseus Parnther

How To Apply For Scholarships In 5 Easy Steps

Shedly Casseus Parnther

How To Apply For Scholarships In 5 Easy Steps

Shedly Casseus Parnther

How To Apply For Scholarships In 5 Easy Steps

Shedly Casseus Parnther

How To Apply For Scholarships In 5 Easy Steps